D1138505

THE FORGOTTEN TRINITY

*1   The Report of the BCC Study Commission
on Trinitarian Doctrine Today*

The British Council of Churches
Inter-Church House
35–41 Lower Marsh
London SE1 7RL

ISBN 0-85169-114-5

Published by the British Council of Churches
Inter-Church House
35-41 Lower Marsh
London SE1 7RL

Designed by Gooderham Bate
Typeset and printed by Delta Press, Brighton, E. Sussex
22DEA
© 1989 The British Council of Churches

Contents

Preface

This Report is the first of three publications on *The Forgotten Trinity*, the fruits of the BCC Study Commission on Trinitarian Doctrine Today which held ten meetings between November 1983 and May 1988.

In reporting to the churches, the Commission wanted to avoid falling between two stools: that of theological and academic adequacy, and that of accessibility to people in the pew. This could have happened if it had simply produced a report aimed at the average synod or assembly member. Instead it is producing three items:

1. This Report of the BCC Study Commission on Trinitarian Doctrine Today, aimed at a theologically informed audience;

2. A Study Guide on six issues contained in the Commission's Report, aimed at local churches' study groups where people are prepared to do some hard thinking together.

3. A Selection of Papers presented to the Commission, aimed at an academic audience.

At the BCC Autumn 1989 Assembly in London, Assembly members are due to use the Study Guide in groups and debate a resolution commending the work of the Commission to the churches and bringing before their Faith and Order and Church Unity departments the particular issues it contains.

The Division of Ecumenical Affairs wishes to express its gratitude to those who chaired and served on the Study Commission and especially those who drafted and edited the Report, Study Guide, and Selection of Papers.

Alastair Haggart
Moderator, Division of Ecumenical Affairs
June 1989

The members of the BCC Study Commission on Trinitarian Doctrine Today wish to thank the British Council of Churches for the opportunity they have been given to work together and learn from one another over the last six years. They would like particularly to thank Colin Davey, Secretary of the Study Commission, whose contributions, organisational ability and excellent co-ordination of our work have made this Report, as well as the Study Guide and Essays, possible.

Costa Carras
James Torrance
Co-Chairmen

1 Introduction

1. There is a feeling abroad that the doctrine of the Trinity is an irrelevance. Once the centre of fierce debate, it now seems to belong to our religious past, and to have little to say about the great issues of the day. It appears to be a mere abstraction, a playing with mathematical conundrums, of interest simply to those engaged in the higher reaches of theological speculation but of little moment for the worship of the church and the life of the world. Yet the rise in recent years of the charismatic movement with its stress on the work of the Holy Spirit, and the accompanying attention that it has drawn to the existence of Pentecostal churches, raise urgent questions about the significance of differences of trinitarian belief. Indeed, the very institution of the Study Commission in 1983 suggested that dismissal of the matter might be premature.

1.2 The Study Commission was set up as the result of three particular concerns: that of the Russian Orthodox Church in Britain (Diocese of Sourozh) to commemorate the 1600th anniversary of the Council of Constantinople (381 A.D.) by encouraging a fresh examination of its creed by representatives of the British churches together; that of the World Council of Churches for national Councils of Churches to pursue further the questions re-examined in its Faith and Order Study *Spirit of God, Spirit of Christ* (1981); and that of the British Council of Churches and its Division of Ecumenical Affairs to give a greater proportion of its attention to faith and order questions.

1.3 Our work in the years since that time has proved the value of this initiative, for it has become clear to us that on the question of the Trinity centre numerous matters of great moment. At the heart of them is the question of who is the God whom Christians worship and serve. From that centre radiate other equally important questions. What are we doing when we worship God? Does our understanding of God have any implications for how we regard and treat the world? Christians, along with many who do not profess Christian belief, have always spoken of 'creation' and 'salvation'. Does belief in the three-in-oneness of God have any implications for the way we understand them? Again, a question at the centre of debate now is that of the nature of the human person, including the matter of male and female. What is the relation of the doctrine of the Trinity to this contemporary debate? Of similar importance are discussions of the nature of the Church and its relation to culture, including political culture; of ecumenical relationships as well as those between Christians and members of other religious communities; and of the relation of contemporary Christianity to our religious past, particularly its relation to modernity and the questions it raises about the authority and interpretation of Scripture. All of these matters entered into the discussions of the Study Commission, some of them more prominently than others. The following report attempts to bring the main themes together in such a way as to do justice both to the questions asked of the Commission and to the main direction of our enquiries.

2 Where We Stand

2.1 **Worship in the Church.** We believe that as members of the Church of God we stand before and with the God made known as Father, Son and Holy Spirit. The primary form of this relationship is our worship, in which we are brought to God the Father through his Son and in his Spirit. In this way it is given to us to participate in the self-offering and prayer of Christ our great high priest. Worship is above all the act of the Christian community, in which God enables his people, in all their human diversity, to realise that communion with their creator and with each other without which they are not truly human. Worship in the Spirit is truly our worship, but it does not originate in ourselves. The promise of Romans 8, for example, is that 'we do not know how to pray as we ought' (v.26), but that we are graciously caught up into a divine conversation. 'The Spirit bears witness with our spirit' (v.16), interceding for us and directing our minds to Christ 'who ever lives to intercede' for us (Hebrews 7.25). There are various ways in which the trinitarian character of worship has been and is understood: as being offered to the Father through the Son and in the Spirit; or to the Father, to the Son and to the Spirit; or to the one triune God. But all alike witness to the reality of relationship, of communion. The communion of Christians with God and with each other is both symbolised and realised in the sacraments of baptism and the eucharist. Baptism is universally administered in the Church in the threefold name of Father, Son and Holy Spirit, and by it we are initiated into the community of God's people. The theme of baptism is of great importance in this context, because it opens out other aspects also of the theology of the Trinity. The baptism of Jesus has long been regarded in the Church as a revelation of the Triune God. According to the biblical witness, the Father there both affirms the Sonship of Jesus and sends the Spirit to empower his ministry. Similarly, in the eucharist, there is prayer to God the Father to send the Holy Spirit that Christ may be present with his people in worship, and that we might share with him his communion with the Father. The Holy Spirit lifts God's people into the presence of the Father as he brings the risen Christ into their midst, and through him enables them to offer to God both themselves and the life of the whole creation in thanksgiving and praise.

2.1.2 As our work has progressed, we have come to realise more and more the importance of the trinitarian basis of the worship and life of the Church. We have therefore begun the body of our report with a confession (2.1), because we wish to enclose everything else that we say within a statement of what we believe to be the most fundamental reality: 'where we stand' is before the triune God in worship and praise. But we also stand in the modern Western world, which has in recent centuries experienced profound disturbances in the pattern of its life and thought, disturbances which have thrown many past certainties into question. As we proceed to examine the reasons why the centrality of the doctrine of the Trinity is one of those things called into question, we do not wish to deny our opening confession, but to work through the questions to a new and firmer apprehension of the importance of our topic.

2.2 **Contemporary Considerations.** It is widely held that despite the lip-service that continues to be paid, the doctrine of the Trinity is in many parts of the Church a dead letter in life and worship. The evidence for such a belief is, however, inconclusive. A small sociological survey, prepared for this Commission, of church members in parts of North London produced a wide range of responses, but did at least suggest that worshippers do believe the matter to be important. A similar survey of recent theological literature would appear to be equally inconclusive. Indeed, it can be argued that there are two powerful contemporary theological streams, operating in parallel although with some mutual influence: the one indifferent or hostile to trinitarian theology, the other consciously locating itself within the mainstream Christian tradition, and finding the heart of that tradition to be in its trinitarian understanding of God.

2.2.2 Whether or not this is the case, there is a number of factors which might be expected to have caused a decline in the trinitarian character of worship, theology and life today. They are all in some way related to major intellectual movements characteristic of modern culture, so that even to raise the question about the Trinity enmeshes us in wide-ranging debate about the nature of Christianity in the modern world. First, it has always been apparent that trinitarian doctrine cannot be simply read off the pages of Scripture; but modern critical study of the Bible has tended to argue for the 'secondary' nature of many of those texts which are most explicitly trinitarian, and this has led some to call into question the legitimacy of the entire doctrinal development which resulted in the full doctrine of the Trinity. Second, an important factor in contemporary doubts about the Trinity is the experiential dimension of modern theology since Schleiermacher. Here it is contended that, while we may in some way or other experience a threeness of God in life or worship, such experience does not license traditional speculation about the being of God in himself. Third, there is pressure from contemporary movements which are influential in the Church, prominently feminism. The way that the three persons of the Trinity have been understood is sometimes held to engender a heavily patriarchal and authoritarian conception of the deity. Fourth, it is also argued that Christian trinitarian belief presents an obstacle to conversation with members of other religious communities, and that it would therefore be expedient to reduce emphasis on this aspect of our beliefs.

2.2.3 On the other hand, it is also possible to report something of a renaissance in the theology of the Trinity in recent times, and, indeed, in all the main streams of the Christian Church. In 1932 the first volume of Karl Barth's *Church Dogmatics* placed the doctrine of the Trinity at the head of Christian theology and gave a new focus to all areas of theological thought. The treatise on the Trinity owed debts both to St Augustine and to the Eastern tradition of trinitarian thought. In 1944, Vladimir Lossky's *The Mystical Theology of the Eastern Church* stressed the distinctive marks of the Eastern approach over against the West's, and so gave impetus to ecumenical debate which still continues. In 1967 Karl Rahner's *The Trinity*, which reflected the influence of Barth, sought to recall the Catholic tradition to its trinitarian roots. The influence of all three of these works continues, and there have been numerous more recent writings. Represented in the Appendix are works by Roman Catholic, Orthodox, Anglican, Lutheran, Methodist and Reformed theologians, writing from Britain, America and mainland Europe.

2.3 **Historical Considerations.** A study such as ours takes place in the context not only of contemporary concerns but also of the historical past which shapes the way the considerations listed in 2.2.2 are received and understood. The culture we call modern is at least in part a response to Western mediaeval Christendom, while that in turn represented one of the forms taken by Christianity in the centuries after the patristic era. Many contemporary doubts about the doctrine of the Trinity took shape in the early modern reaction against mediaeval Christianity, a reaction which was often consciously rationalist and deist in direction. But it can also be argued that Western trinitarianism has declined partly under the weight of its own inadequacies, particularly in the minimal place it has given to the doctrine of the Holy Spirit.

2.3.2 Accordingly, a historical factor of dominating concern during the Study Commission's meetings, attended as they have been by representatives of both East and West, has been the parting of the ways between the two traditions. The theological basis of the schism lies in some measure in the differences between the Cappadocian formulation of the Trinity and that of St Augustine. Representatives of the Eastern tradition, although not they alone, have been strongly critical of the mainstream Western development, for reasons which will be rehearsed later in the Report. By way of anticipation, it may be said here that underlying all discussions of the *Filioque* (see below, 5.2) – where the differences between the traditions come to credal expression – are important differences in the ways in which the two traditions worship, think and live. Here again the place of the doctrine of the Holy Spirit comes into prominence. The matter, however, is very complex, because there are important differences within the two traditions as well as overlap between them.

2.3.3 An even more complex picture of the historical background is presented by studies of the trinitarian content and dimensions of liturgy and hymnody. If it is true that recent liturgical revisions in the West have made the liturgy less trinitarian, it may be that they are in that respect developing ancient tendencies in that area of Christendom rather than merely introducing novelty. Thus one of our papers observed of the modern language eucharistic rite of the Church of England's *Alternative Service Book* that with the exception of the eucharistic prayer it 'is effectively binitarian since the Holy Spirit is only mentioned in the Gloria (optional), the Creed, an optional introduction to the Peace, an optional final collect and the Blessing'. But the same writer also commented that 'in the (1662) Prayer Book few collects mention the Holy Spirit in their conclusions.' The roots of recent anti-trinitarianism may in fact lie far back in early times, and represent not merely a modern development, but one which was prepared by the logic of ancient debate. And yet it must be admitted that other evidence introduces a contrast, and shows that the matter is more complicated than a straightforward reading of such evidence may suggest. An examination of hymnody – the liturgical framework for many Free Church traditions – revealed that many hymns in modern use, both ancient and more recent, are strongly marked by trinitarian language and themes, and their influence on popular belief and practice may be considerable.

2.3.4 The historical background would, therefore, appear to give some, though not unanimous, support to the picture of the present position sketched in 2.2. The doctrine of the Trinity has deeply marked theology and worship, but there are also indications that it is not so determinative as may sometimes be supposed. If the Trinity has declined from the centre of church life in the West, it is in large measure the outcome of the process of criticism of which we are the heirs. But that process operated within a tradition which already displayed what appear to be inherent weaknesses. These weaknesses have emerged in different aspects of the Study Commission's enquiry, and will be pointed out below. It would appear that much depends upon the way in which the doctrine of the Holy Spirit has been developed and understood in worship, theology and life. Before, however, such matters can be treated directly, there must be some further specification of the process of criticism, and of how it has operated to raise doubts from within the Christian tradition about the reliability of the basis upon which its doctrinal formulations have been constructed.

2.4 Biblical Criticism and the Foundations of the Doctrine of the Trinity. There is no doubt that a major reason for modern doubts about the validity of the doctrine of the Trinity is to be found in that kind of critical and historical study of the biblical text which began with the humanism of the Renaissance and gained new impetus in the Reformation and Enlightenment. In the early years of this century it was vigorously argued that the early christological and trinitarian formulations represented the Hellenization of Christianity, by which was meant a process whereby the teaching of Jesus or the basic Christian gospel was both unnecessarily complicated and at least partially distorted by the imposition upon it of foreign philosophical concepts. It is now generally agreed that this approach was an oversimplification. But it did establish that the relation between the biblical and patristic teaching is not such a simple one as used to be supposed.

2.4.2 This approach seemed to bear particularly hard on the doctrine of the Trinity, in that in any case there are few biblical texts which can be claimed to have an explicitly trinitarian significance. Modern critical study has certainly sharpened this difficulty by demonstrating that many of those passages which do appear to support the doctrine of the Trinity belong to later stages of the New Testament tradition. The command, for example, to baptise 'in the name of the Father and of the Son and of the Holy Spirit' (Matthew 28.19) is now widely held not to report the actual words of Jesus but to reflect early baptismal practice. Again, it is no accident (it is said) that some of the most significant 'trinitarian' texts occur in St. John's Gospel, particularly those which describe the work of the Paraclete in relation to the Father and the Son (John 14.15ff; 16.7ff); for this Gospel is held to represent a late stage in the reflection of the Church compared with the much more primitive and less obviously trinitarian material in the Synoptic Gospels. Moreover, it is not just a case of particular proof texts. Modern studies of St Paul's theology have often argued that not only does he not always clearly distinguish between the risen Christ and the Spirit, but that at times he refers to them interchangeably as if he was aware of no clear distinction between them. Indeed the tendency of biblical scholars today (in contrast to the concern to construct a single 'biblical theology', which was popular only a few decades ago) is to stress the diversity of sometimes incompatible 'theologies' which may be found within the New Testament itself. Given the diversity, it has understandably been asked how any single doctrine can any longer be claimed to be securely based in 'the teaching of the Bible'.

2.4.3 Underlying this critique of the traditional basis for doctrinal formulations is of course a presupposition that has usually been associated with, but is not necessary to, the historical-critical method, namely, that the most important object of our quest is that which is oldest and most 'primitive' in the tradition, and that the late strands in the New Testament can be virtually disregarded as 'secondary'. Given that (as we have noted) the few explicitly trinitarian texts belong for the most part in this category, the doctrine of the Trinity might seem particularly vulnerable to this approach. But in fact this is by no means the end of the story. Consider, for example, the relation of christology to the New Testament evidence when subjected to the scrutiny of modern critical study. According to this, the texts which seem to affirm the divinity of Christ are few and far between, belong to the latest writings of the New Testament, are occasionally textually uncertain (see John 1.18) and are in every case capable of more than one interpretation: 'Son of God' can be shown to be a title which in the time of Christ did not necessarily imply divine status; 'Son of Man' may have been no more than a colloquial idiom and 'Messiah' have implied nothing superhuman. Moreoever there is a great diversity between different New Testament writings in their approach to the nature and status of Christ, and no single christology could ever be claimed to enjoy the support of the entire New Testament. However, even if all these conclusions are accepted, nevertheless it by no means follows even for the majority of New Testament scholars, that the Church must have been wrong or unjustified in arriving so soon at a clear faith in the divinity of Christ. For the diverse and sometimes competing christological formulations in the New Testament at least attest to a continuing sense of the reality of the risen Christ and an inextinguishable urge to find adequate words in which to worship and proclaim him.

The same is true of that perception and experience of God which was to result in the doctrine of the Trinity. Here what is earliest is not necessarily normative. The development from the inchoate and sometimes barely compatible affirmations in the Bible to the later trinitarian formulations was not just a matter of logical inference from certain texts, a process which might now be judged to have been incorrect or inadequate. Rather, this development occurred within a complex matrix of experience and reflection. It arose from the Church's participation in the life of God, a participation granted by the Spirit and therefore requiring both the divinity of the Spirit and his distinction from the Father; and from her sending out into all the world, a mission deriving from the mission of the Son. This matrix provides the clue to the coherence of the diverse strands of New Testament evidence, and provided essential continuity with the developments which were to come. It is our ultimate justification for treating the biblical evidence, not just as a historical record which may be analysed, dated and evaluated by modern critical methods, but as prime evidence for that continual pressure to articulate the experience of faith, worship and mission which was to achieve a satisfying formulation only in a later century.

2.4.4 However much, therefore, we may be prepared to agree that a doctrine of the Trinity cannot be simply read off the text of Scripture or based directly upon certain biblical texts, we can continue to affirm that the God who is made known in the Old and New Testaments is the triune God confessed in later worship and in the teaching of the Church. Nothing in modern historical criticism forces us to deny a true continuity between the way in which God is known in the Old Testament, is named in threefold form in the New Testament and is defined in trinitarian terms through the maturing of insights made possible by the ministry, death and resurrection of Jesus as well as by life in the Spirit in the Church. The meaning of Scripture is not exhausted by historical and critical study. Earlier passages adumbrate later ones in a way that the Church has always felt impelled to attribute to the providential guidance of the Holy Spirit; and a full interpretation must take account of what we have called the matrix of the worship, reflection and mission of the Church.

2.4.5 But what is the matrix in which today's discussion of trinitarian theology takes place? We would hold that it is wrong to assume that the modern experience of God is so different from that of the past that our teaching cannot be continuous with the ancient. There are differences, but the belief that there is an unbridgeable gulf between ancient and modern experience is one that should be put to the test, not assumed. Whether such a gulf is a reality cannot be decided simply, and much will depend upon the outcome of the argument of the whole of this report. The chief thing to be said in anticipation of our conclusions is that the large majority of the group's members do not accept that there is such a difference between ancient and modern experience of the world and of God. In any case, we do wish to warn against the kind of 'chronological snobbery' (C.S. Lewis) that is so easy for the modern age, when we believe that we can automatically assume our superiority to and dismissive criticism of the theological legacy of the past. Not only that, but more positively we would affirm it is one of the gifts of the Holy Spirit to rescue us from an overestimation of our own wisdom and an undervaluing of what we receive from the tradition.

2.4.6 Indeed, it is at this point that we would argue that the appeal to experience cuts another way. Once we are freed by the Spirit from an over-estimation of one culture – our own – and one way of approaching the Scriptures, we are able to open ourselves anew to the experience of the historic Christian community. We shall find, when we do, that the wisdom of the ages has much to give us, and that the doctrine of the Trinity is not irrelevant to many of the modern questions which we are tempted to assume are more important than a dogma coming to us from our past. Quite the reverse, for such questions as those of the significance of the person, of the meaning of life on earth, of society, politics and justice take on new meaning when treated in a trinitarian dimension. Above all, we would argue that discussion of the being of God is not simply an abstract matter, for it has to do with the truth, and therefore with the integrity of the Christian tradition and Church. It is to this first substantive question that we shall proceed.

3 God

Two features of our theological history affect, and perhaps distort, the way we approach the question of the existence and nature of God. The first has been indicated by Karl Rahner, in the book to which reference has already been made, where he says that traditional treatments of the questions have tended to hold apart discussions of the oneness of God and of his threeness. That can easily lead us to believe that, because the treatment of God's unity sets and dominates the scene, the threeness has little to show us of what God really is. And so we remain 'almost just monotheist'. Because the Trinity is not treated as essential to an understanding of the being of God, it tends to be treated as an afterthought, more or less optional for theology. The second is that when we do approach the doctrine of the Trinity, we tend to do so rather one-sidedly in the light of christology. We thus come to be dominated by a Father-Son pattern of thinking, and so lose or relegate to relative unimportance the place of the Holy Spirit. Yet if 'where we stand' is in worship before the Father, through the Son, indeed, but also in the Spirit, is not such an impoverishment to be if possible avoided? If our theology is to be rooted in our worship of God, we shall seek to transcend the narrowing by which both our worship and our thought lose the richness bequeathed to us by our trinitarian heritage. In this chapter we shall, then, seek to indicate something of the importance of the doctrine of the Trinity for both worship and thought. But, as we found in the previous chapter, 'where we stand' is also at the end of a process of development which has raised our question in a particular way, from christology. Because christology and the doctrine of the Trinity are inextricably linked we shall begin there, with the christological concentration of recent times, and attempt to show both its weaknesses and its possibilities for trinitarian transformation.

3.1. **Jesus and God.**   Recent treatment of the theme of the relation of Jesus and God has been dominated, as has much recent biblical interpretation, by questions of historicity. What can we know of Jesus? Even if there are facts that can be discovered, what basis do they offer for a theology? These are typical of the questions which have dominated, for better or worse, recent critical discussion, particularly in Britain. Much of this questioning is directed to the status of Jesus as distinctively or uniquely making present and revealing the eternal God. Here a wide range of interpretations is possible, from those which hold that Jesus is in some way a symbol of or pointer to a God who is other than he, through various mediating positions to a full blown teaching of the incarnation. Almost all of the members of the Study Commission hold to an incarnational christology of a fairly traditional form. It is important to be aware of the fact that, whatever position is taken, there is a close relation between beliefs about the person of Christ and beliefs about other things, particularly those about God and the world. If it is held that Jesus is God incarnate, it is likely also to be believed that God is triune in himself and that he interrelates actively with the world. A large part of the Study Commission's time has been spent on this question and its ramifications, for the reason that so much else depends upon it. We begin with the clarification of its meaning, and move from there to its wider implications.

3.1.2 A major question for the orthodox trinitarian tradition of both East and West concerns the relation of the human Jesus to the eternal Word or Son of God. One of the traditions of ancient christological thinking, that centred on Alexandria, stressed the significance of the person of Christ as the incarnation of the eternal Son. When it was asked why their stress on the movement of God into time did not deprive Jesus of his true humanity, an answer was developed which argued that it is the Word who constitutes Jesus' humanity as human. His humanity is the humanity of the Word. The question of what this can mean is important because underlying it are a number of others. Chief among them is the matter of the involvement of God in our human condition. It has been the shared belief of all parts of the Christian tradition that if God is not involved in the humanity of Jesus, there is no salvation. The character of the salvation brought or realised in Jesus has been interpreted differently in East and West, with the West tending to concentrate on sin and forgiveness, the East on the human sharing in the divine life; but both have asserted the centrality of the divine action in time. Some recent trinitarian writings have added to this a note of theodicy, proclaiming an involvement of the Father in the suffering of Jesus, the crucified God, as God's saving sharing of our alienation. Differences between these views indicate differences of emphasis and conception of the human need or plight met by the action of God, but not any real disagreement about the centrality of Jesus to the process.

3.1.3 A second question arising from the traditional teaching that Christ's humanity is that of the Word concerns the authenticity of such a humanity. Historical critical questioning in recent times has suggested that traditional conceptions fail to do justice to the human figure portrayed in the Gospels. This, too, is a question with implications for trinitarian theology. Theology has tended to underplay the humanity of Christ. It has not done so in theory, because it has argued, as we have seen, that his humanity is maintained as such because of its relation to the Word: it is the humanity of the Word and for this reason truly human. Yet it must be doubted whether that alone is enough to ensure the full humanity of Jesus, because it can so easily appear that the human actions are overridden by the divine agency of the Word. The appeal of modern 'kenotic' christologies which stress the self-emptying of the eternal Word in the incarnation derives from the fact that they seem to do far greater justice to the humanity of Jesus. On the traditional account, however, the question recurs of whether we still have the human figure presented by the Gospels. Similarly, the Western teaching that the Spirit 'proceeds from the Father and the Son' (*Filioque*) tends to place excessive stress on Christ as the giver of the Spirit, and would help to explain the 'docetic' strain in some traditional theology. We do not wish to deny the traditional teaching that Jesus' humanity is the humanity of the Word, but wish to counterbalance it with an emphasis that is equally important. The narratives of Jesus' birth show that the authentic humanity of Jesus is the gift of the Holy Spirit. The fact that in his baptism he is the recipient of the Spirit affirms what he shares with us alongside that in which, as Lord, he is different from us.

3.2 **Incarnation and Trinity.** There are then two sides to the significance of Jesus as the incarnate Word. On the one hand, because his origin is in God, human salvation is seen to be rooted in eternity, in the eternal goodness of the creator. On the other hand, because Jesus is a genuine human being, maintained in truth by the Holy Spirit, salvation is not realised over our heads in some timeless eternity but takes shape in a human way in our experience in time and space. But even where that teaching is accepted, its implications for the Christian understanding of God are controversial. To speak of God's presence and activity in Jesus is to speak about something that happens, as we have seen, in time and space. Technically, this has been referred to as the divine 'economy': God's dispensation (*oeconomia*) for and in the world, the temporal and historical interaction of God with the world. It is a further step to argue that such speech licenses us to speak about what has traditionally been called the 'immanent' Trinity, in which we claim to be able to say something about what God is in himself and for ever. How important is it that the step should be taken?

3.2.2 Here again we encounter historical legacies, which have left the impression in many minds that traditional ways of specualating about the inner being of God have both proceeded far beyond what the evidence allows and have in any case been pointless exercises from the point of view of human worship and life. The result is that a gulf has often opened up between the Trinity made known in the economy and the inner trinitarian being of God, so that concern with the latter appears an irrelevance. We believe that such considerations as this may underlie much recent distaste for trinitarian theologizing.

3.2.3 Another reason for the suspicion with which the tradition is sometimes faced is that it sometimes appears to be too familiar with the inner life of God, too certain that its concepts are able to grasp the essence of the divine. We believe that theology at its best has never succumbed to temptation in so gross a way, but the suspicion does allow us to voice a salutary reminder. Theological concepts, like other human attempts to grasp the structure of reality, necessarily fall short of their objects, and this is particularly true of those which attempt to express something of the reality of God. In any case, theologians must always remember that our concern is not merely with solving rational problems; and trinitarian theologians should be particularly aware that persons come before concepts. Theological language is designed to serve the Gospel, the good news of God's love in Christ; and trinitarian language to anchor human worship, life and thought in the way that love takes shape in the 'economy'.

3.2.4 The most disturbing feature of the way that trinitarian theology has sometimes worked is seen in the way that divisions have been imported by it into our expressions of God's action in the world. In the Bible apparent distinctions between the saving work of Christ and the liberating action of the Spirit need not imply any division between the persons. Father, Son and Spirit are related in such a way that the work of one is the work of all. There is, for example, a oneness of mind between the Father and the Son, revealed particularly in the cross, in their common concern to bring many children to glory. Sometimes, however, the matter has been put in such a way that the work of Father and Son is separated, so that, for example, it sometimes appears as if on the cross Jesus is being punished by the Father. (The question of what we mean by calling God 'Father' will concern us later in the Report). This dualism, or holding apart of what should be held together, appears in other spheres as well. The impression has sometimes been given that, far from enabling the world and human life to be themselves, God is the enemy of human freedom, so that there is competition between God and the world, and in order to be free we must rebel. Again, this is far from the biblical picture of the Spirit's setting free of human beings by bringing them to the Father through Christ. Some of the worst effects of such a dualistic way of thought have been experienced in worship, where a 'Pelagian' conception often holds sway. Instead of experiencing worship in a trinitarian way, as an event in which the people of God are lifted up to the Father by the Spirit through the Son, so that worship is both something enabled by God and truly human, the stress has come to be on something that we do by ourselves.

3.2.5 In view of the problems which have been outlined, it is noteworthy that some recent approaches to Trinitarian doctrine have attempted to escape the abstractness and tendency to dualism by bringing the economic and immanent trinities into closer relation. Notable among the contributions are those of:

(1) Karl Barth, who wished to root any talk about who God is in himself in his historical revelation in Jesus. Reasserting an ancient tradition, he argued that God is eternally in himself what he reveals himself to be in Jesus Christ. Working 'back' from revelation – or economy – to inner being he holds that whatever is true about God's triune ways towards us must also be true of what he is in himself, eternally. Thus he seeks to unite in thought God's being and his act. Barth's formulation has been influential and his linking of the economy and the being of God is similar to that of

(2) Karl Rahner, who wished to repair what he believed to be a dangerous weakness of conventional Catholic theology which introduced a gulf between the oneness and the threeness of God. His dictum 'the immanent trinity is the revealed trinity' is much quoted and discussed, but was not intended to create an absolute identity of the two. Rather, he was concerned to correct the method of theology in the light of the principle that 'the triune God is the primal ground of the history of salvation.' The impulses of Barth and Rahner are carried further by

(3) Jürgen Moltmann, whose emphasis is social and political. Moltmann affirms that the doctrine of the Trinity provides us with the matrix for a new kind of thinking about God, the world and humankind. The doctrine of the Trinity is for him a way of speaking about the openness of God to the world and of the openness of the world to the future God has for it.

All of these recent expositions are concerned to give some place to the doctrine of God's eternal or inner being, but to prevent the kind of abstract and independent speculation about it that has sometimes taken place in the tradition. They are in different ways influenced by strands of thought deriving from the Eastern Orthodox tradition. One of the concerns of the Study Commission has been whether and to what extent there is any point in developing a theology of the being of God in himself. A major focus of our discussion has been the question of being. Some of our contributors have argued that our understanding of the nature of the world and of ourselves as part of it is bound up with the kind of reality that we believe God to be.

3.3 **The Indispensability of the Doctrine of the Immanent Trinity.** What is implied by the teaching that God is what he is as three persons in relation? The chief lesson is that if God is essentially relational, then all being shares in relation: there is, that is to say, a relational content built into the notion of being. To be is to exist in relation to other beings. Christian theology took shape in a world where it was believed that the foundations for the world were provided by an impersonal substructure of being which was *logically* related to the superstructure. By contrast, in the doctrine of the Trinity the Fathers developed a conception of being at the heart of which were not logical but *personal* relations. They were able to do this because the pressure on their thought of belief in Jesus and the Spirit led them to conceive of a God whose *being* consisted in communion. God is a community consisting in unbroken personal relationships. This was a new and unique contribution to thought, and enabled all aspects of human life to be conceived in a new way. But it did not take place in a vacuum, and can from one point of view be understood as the coming together of the Jewish and Hellenic worlds, with Jewish ways of thinking about God in personal terms being developed with the aid of conceptuality borrowed and adapted from the context in which the worship and life of the Church took shape. The implications of the development were revolutionary, for they entail, for example, that the world is not the product of some impersonal, mechanistic or logical process but the creation of a free and personal God. If the being of God consists in personal communion, it implies the priority of the personal over all other dimensions of being. In that sense, trinitarian theology has implications for all spheres of our life, some of which are reviewed in the body of this report.

3.3.2 One aspect of the development which can be mentioned here is that of monotheism. It is sometimes asserted that Christianity is a monotheistic religion; sometimes, that monotheism is a subchristian distortion. One theologian, Erik Peterson, writing during the Nazi era, argued that monotheism can provide the basis for absolutist and totalitarian political and social orders (See below, 6.2). Much depends upon what is meant by the oneness of God. If it is a purely mathematical oneness, there is a return to impersonal monism, in which personal values are swallowed in the impersonal. By contrast, the Trinity is concerned with the relational oneness which has already been mentioned. In turn, however, this raises important questions which have to be faced. Does it make relations with other religions, whether monotheistic or not, easier or more difficult? That question will require separate treatment (below, 6.4). At this stage, we are concerned primarily to set out the kind of framework for thought about the world which is made available by the tradition of trinitarian thinking. We now move from framework to detail with the discussion of a matter which has been at the heart of the Commission's work.

4 The Person

4.1 **Individualism.** Laments about the 'individualism' of the modern world are often heard; at the same time, and often from the same quarters, much is made of the disappearance of the individual in the impersonal mass, whether the mass be modern 'consumerist' society or totalitarian regimes of various kinds. It is sometimes also pointed out that the desperate quest for 'relationship' that characterises modern societies is the outcome of a loss of the person: people are, by the nature of our society, cut off from their fellows and must seek for what they do not have. Even here, the response is all too often to seek individual self-fulfilment rather than the creation of genuine community. It is in such areas as these that the Study Commission has found its greatest unanimity. The doctrine of the Trinity is the source of personal values which enable us to transcend some of the sterilities of current social debate.

4.1.2 The chief source of our problems is the pervasive individualism of the Western tradition. Some of us believe that the problem goes at least as far back as Augustine and, indeed, his formulation of the doctrine of the Trinity. Because he came to seek the image of God in the threefold structure of the individual human mind, rather than, say, in the *relatedness* of one human person to another, and because of his dominating influence on all subsequent theology, he made it difficult for those who followed him to break out of his framework and call upon the insights of other thinkers. Whether that be fair, and, as we shall see there are other important contributions of a less individualistic character to be found in the Western tradition, it is certainly true that since Descartes, the philosophical mainstream has virtually equated the person with the individual. The chief focus of recent debate has been on whether the person is primarily a mind or a body, rather than on that presupposed in the title of a work not in the mainstream, John Macmurray's *Persons in Relation*. The ominous outcome is to be read in Derek Parfit's recent *Reasons and Persons*, which appears to wish to dispense with the notion of person altogether. It is ominous because it can only reinforce the already considerable threat to personal values in the modern world.

4.1.3 The development of the concept of the person, in so far as there is one, in sociology follows a similar course. The founding fathers of sociology, Durkheim for example, tended to develop or encourage a purely functional view of the person, although the same cannot be said of Weber. The weakness is particularly to be found in the successors of Comte for whom persons entirely disappear into normative social roles. Marx's earlier writings promise much in view of his critique of post-Enlightenment individualism: individual persons would be free only (would become subjects not objects) when they could recognise each other as members of a universal social being. Yet he has no real notion of personhood, except, perhaps, in an eschatological sense: for him, personhood arrives only when socialism as the apotheosis of human history arrives. More recent sociological writing has little more to contribute, despite some signs of increased interest. The word *person* does not appear in the index of the fourteen volumes of the *International Encyclopedia of Social Science* published up to 1985. The conclusion would appear to be that although it may be claimed that theology requires the insights offered by modern sociology, the reverse is equally true: that theology must contribute its own distinctive trinitarian insights if debate in other disciplines is to be adequate.

4.2 **The Trinity and the Person.** The concept of the person has a history not only in secular philosophical thought, but in discussions of the doctrine of the Trinity. Here, however, it is also problematic, because it has been the source of much difficulty. It is to be noted that Augustine was unsure what use to make of the concept in his treatise on the Trinity, and in the end concluded that he must use it only 'in order not to remain silent'. Its place in the doctrine of God has since been called into question and this may be because *person* has so often appeared to be the equivalent of *individual*. It would be absurd and tritheistic to say that God is three individuals, and would give substance to the charges of those – Muslims, for example – who say that Christians believe in three gods. It was for such reasons that Barth, believing that the word inevitably suggested 'three centres of consciousness', individualistically conceived, suggested the abandonment of the word *person* in connection with God's threeness, and preferred to speak of three mutually related modes (or ways) of being of the one personal God. In so doing, he was attempting to mediate between the Eastern and Western traditions, for the expression is borrowed from the Cappadocian Fathers, who used both the term *person* and the term *mode of being* in an ontological and not a psychological sense. The matter is of immense complexity, but its importance for the concept of the person can be realised if we state the chief questions that arise from Barth's formulation.

(i) Does it necessarily follow that to speak of three centres of consciousness is to imply the existence of three separate (rather than distinct) beings, and so of three gods? Should we not rather say that whatever else we say of God, we should not make him less than we are, and deny to the persons who constitute the Godhead the consciousness that is often taken to be one of the marks of human excellence? May it not be that the 'consciousnesses' of Father, Son and Holy Spirit are distinct but exist only in the *perichoresis*, the interanimation, the mutual giving and receiving that makes the divine persons what they are only in their relations to each other? On the other hand, may it not rather be argued against such a speculation that to speak in such a way is to be anthropomorphic, naively importing what we take to be important into the being of God, and that it is better not to indulge in speculation of this kind?

(ii) Barth argues that the concept of the personality of God is better used in connection with the unity than with the threeness of God. The question here is whether to do so is to underwrite individualism. Does this necessarily suggest that God is an individual in the bad sense of that word; or is it an essential safeguard against any suggestion that there are three gods, as well as an attempt to reach out to a concept of person-hood more adequate to God? The feeling of many of the members of the Commission, however, is that such an approach places too much stress on unity over against the necessary emphasis on the interrelation-ship of persons, but we do wish to call attention to the fact that the West has always been aware of the importance of showing that the person-hood of God, even when conceived in a unitary way, must not be con-ceived in an individualist sense. In order to emphasize God's personal complexity, Augustine and later theologians developed the concept of a person as a 'subsistent relation'. It must be said that members of the Study Commission were divided in their evaluation of this, many of us holding that it is inadequate because it appears to dissolve persons into relationships, whereas we hold that relationships are between persons.

4.2.2 Whatever answers are given to each of those related questions, it can be seen that there is a common concern underlying them. Much of the work of the Commission was concerned with the discussion of what resources there are, in the treatment of the concept of the person in trinitarian theology, for a conception of the person which is not indi-vidualistic and therefore will help to underwrite a genuinely social or communitarian conception of human being. Such a conception should meet two requirements. On the one hand, it should preserve the particularity and uniqueness of every person; on the other, it should not oppose this particularity to social relationships, but would show how the being of the particular derives from its relatedness to other particu-lars.

4.2.3 There was remarkable unanimity in the Study Commission in looking for resources to the three Cappadocian Fathers, St Gregory

Nazianzen, St Gregory of Nyssa and St Basil of Caesarea, as well as to some Latin thinkers such as Tertullian, St Hilary of Poitiers and Richard of St Victor. Here is to be found a corrective to the relative one-sidedness of the later Western tradition and its tendency to encourage individualism. The basis of the theological contribution to the concept of the person is to be found in the fact that, under pressure of the Christian Gospel and in the light of their particular concerns, the Cappadocian Fathers developed a new conception of what it is *to be*. The trinitarian conception of God is, said St Basil of Caesarea, 'a new and paradoxical conception of united separation and separated unity.' The being of God is a *relational* unity: it consists in the fact that it is a communion, a being in which the persons give to and receive from each other what they are. When such a conception is used to throw light on created personhood, it will be seen to generate neither an individualist nor a collectivist conception of the person. *Particularity* is at the heart of what is given and received, but, rather than being the denial of social relations, it is in fact its basis, because reciprocity and relationship are present from the outset and not tacked on as an extra. The conception is also characteristically modern in the fact that it can be understood in terms of freedom. To be a person on this account is to be what one gives to and receives freely from the other persons with whom one is in relation. It is also to be noted that, unlike many individualistic modern conceptions of the person rooted in reason or consciousness, it does not exclude – for example – the mentally handicapped from personhood: like other persons, they too are what they are in giving and receiving, although the particular content of their giving and receiving will differ from that of others.

4.2.4 As we saw to be the case with the thought of Marx (4.1.3), there is for theology, too, an eschatological dimension to the concept of the person. In fact, *person* can be claimed to be an essentially eschatological concept, in that true personhood will be realised only in the final Kingdom of God. The nature of the concept enables us to acknowledge that under present historical, material and social conditions, our personhood is less than fully realised. Yet in saying that, we are not being merely abstract, positing a state that is to be realised in some supposed future age alone, for we believe that God in Christ gives us a foretaste of that which will be. Human personhood is realisable in the present through the Spirit in the Church and in other forms of true community. We are thus enabled to say that true personhood is the gift of God. Our relation to God, accordingly, is to be understood in terms of our relation to Jesus and the Spirit. In this connection, something of the significance of baptism can be realised, for it shows us in practice that human identity is created not through our 'natural' relationships, but is grounded in the prior trinitarian community. Such considerations lead us into questions of Trinity and Church, and these will occupy us in the next chapter.

4.3 **The Trinity and Christian Anthropology.** Beliefs about God have always been related to beliefs about what it is to be a human being, and therefore trinitarian teaching has undoubtedly had some effect on the way in which anthropological thought has developed. Yet it must be said that the drawing of explicit links has been somewhat neglected, and that we owe a debt to modern thought in reminding us both of our neglect and in bringing to the attention of theology the importance of the topic. It could be said that the strongly anthropological concentration of thought since the Enlightenment is itself a reaction against and a reflection on the Church's failure to give a satisfactory account of the problem of human freedom. The failure is not as total as is sometimes asserted by unsympathetic critics, because the doctrine of the image of God has played some part in the development of Christian anthropology. And yet there are criticisms to be made of the form which that development took. In the first place, it tended to concentrate on the image as a static characteristic or qualification of the *individual*, and therefore, although it was relational in the sense of being that which relates us to God, it had little directly to say about our relatedness to other human beings. In the second place, by concentrating on reason or freedom or our moral sense as the basis of our distinctive humanity, the tradition has been frequently tempted into an individualist or, indeed, merely secular anthropology: the image of God is that which human beings individually possess. The danger is always that we shall take some creaturely concept and simply project it upon our subject. The effect of an Aristotelian method which imposes a concept of 'the natural' is shown, for example, in what happened in the American Civil War or happens in South Africa, when it is argued that some people are slaves or inferior 'by nature'. Third, by conceiving the image as primarily located in the inner person or mind – as St Augustine influentially did by seeking an analogy for the Trinity in the human mind – there resulted a tendency to produce an over intellectual or idealising conception of the person, neglecting other important dimensions of our createdness, particularly, perhaps, the social and material. On the other hand, it is worth recalling that St Gregory Palamas (1296–1359), for example, taught that the image of God is to be found in the whole person, body, soul and spirit.

4.3.2 There have been, in recent times, some attempts to correct the imbalance, notable among them that of Karl Barth, whose work we introduce as one example of the possibilities and perils inherent in the approach to anthropology we are commending. Barth's anthropology has received much negative criticism in recent times for his adoption of a doctrine of the image of God which continues to see woman as in certain respects subordinate to man. That criticism of Barth, however, should not be allowed to detract from the positive achievement of his anthropology. His work can be said to have a double thrust, the first of which some of us find to be more acceptable than the second. The first is that there is in his theological anthropology much stress on the communal aspects of our reality, and that is important as providing a radical critique of the destructive individualism that is so pervasive in our culture. Barth held that one major development in that direction took place in the thought of Nietzsche, 'the prophet of that humanity without the fellow man . . : the man who is utterly inaccessible to others, having no friends and despising women . . .' Against this Barth developed a trinitarian anthropology, in which relations of reciprocity in the being of God were used to throw light on the human condition. Human beings are those who look each other in the eye, mutually speak to and hear each other, render mutual assistance to each other and do all these things 'with gladness'. 'In its basic form humanity is fellow-humanity'.

4.3.3 The second and more contentious thrust of Barth's work is to be found in his attempt to explore the possibilities for building a trinitarian anthropology by developing the suggestion found in Genesis 1.27. Our being made in the image of the triune God is, on such an understanding, our being created in our co-humanity as male and female. The possibilities in such a development are considerable, but it was criticised by some members of the Commission on the ground that it was wrong to base a theology on what could be understood as merely natural characteristics of our createdness. It offends against the balance of the doctrines of creation and redemption in confusing what we are by nature with what we are as free persons. The argument here is that the important feature is not some natural characteristic, however important, but that we are, as human beings, freely related to each other through and in our otherness. The link to be drawn between the being of God and our own is not in some static and individual possession, but dynamic and relational. As Father, Son and Spirit are God in respect of what they freely give to and receive from each other, so we are human as we share in a like community of free giving and receiving. The image of God, that is to say, is to be found in free community.

4.4 **Summary.** The matter of persons and of personal values is at the heart of our human existence in the world. All around us we see the danger of depersonalisation, because many currents of modern thought and social order threaten the uniqueness of persons and their free relatedness to one another. But it is here, also, that is to be found our greatest opportunity. As we study our history, we find that both 'secular' and trinitarian Christian thought have been interested in the same kind of question, and have over the centuries fertilized each other. On the one hand, we owe the roots of our thought about personhood to early trinitarian developments; on the other, later thought has continued to develop the concepts by which we may understand ourselves and our life in the world. Christians therefore have the opportunity of entering into a conversation with others in the modern world about matters of central concern to us all. Our particular contribution is to draw upon our understanding of the triune God to call attention to particular and central features of our common humanity: our freedom to be with and for each other; our relations which yet respect the otherness, particularity and uniqueness of every human person; and the communion which may be realised through our free and particular relatedness.

5 The Trinity and the Church

5.1 **The Spirit and the Institution.** The doctrine of the Church has not always been treated in very close relation to that of the Holy Spirit. It undoubtedly should have been, but there is little doubt that many of our current ecumenical difficulties derive from past and present fai- to engage deeply with the links between the two. The relation was treated in the thought of St Basil of Caesarea, but after him it tended to be lost, so that discussion was generally limited to questions concerning ministry and sacraments – and even those topics have for the most part been debated in christological terms. Recent theologians to engage with the relation between Trinity and Church are Lossky, Florovsky, Congar, Moltmann and Zizioulas. The Study Commission has spent some time in seeking the reasons for the dissatisfaction with the form the tradition has taken, and in particular has discovered a tendency to abstractness in the way the doctrine of the Spirit has been appealed to as an authority external to the content of the Church's worship and life. We begin therefore with the central matter of worship.

5.1.2 A study of the New Testament and the Fathers revealed to us the rootedness of trinitarian language in the life of prayer and worship. It is evident in St Paul and from the theology of such theologians as Origen and St Basil that the centre of their thought is the dynamic of being brought to the presence of God through Christ by the Holy Spirit. We are 'prayed in' by the Holy Spirit. St Basil is particularly instructive. The entire experience is trinitarian, and St Basil clearly sets out a distinct logic and progression in the roles of each divine person in assimilating the Christian to God. In later Western developments, the matter becomes more abstract, and the 'experiential dynamic' of St Basil's approach appears to be lost. St Augustine, following St Ambrose, finds it difficult to draw a distinction between the activity of the Son and that of the Spirit, and so it becomes simply accepted on authority that there are three 'persons' and that the Spirit must somehow be accounted for as a distinct entity in relation to the other two. Whatever the cause, there has resulted a loss for many modern Christians of the relevance of the Trinity for worship, so that much worship is for practical purposes unitarian, or a transaction between a merely external deity and an autonomous worshipper. Instead of being the worship of our hearts and minds – lifting us out of ourselves to participate in the life of the Godhead – it becomes something that we do, without an awareness of the priesthood of Christ or of the action of the

Spirit. According to such considerations, the difference between the life and death of Christian worship depends upon its recovery of a trinitarian dynamic. The word *dynamic* is important, because we do not wish to suggest that recovery of the truth of worship is merely or even largely a matter of a correct concept of the Trinity. God can work through even the most unpromising structures. What we wish to achieve by our appeal to trinitarian considerations is an undermining of the presumption that in worship we are thrown back on our own resources. We began the body of this report with the statement of our belief that in worship we stand before and with the God made known as Father, Son and Spirit. Here we wish to reiterate that confession, and to add that our concern is not that trinitarian words and phrases should be incorporated in liturgies and hymns in a merely cosmetic way, but that worshippers should celebrate and be drawn into the life and relationships of the triune God. It is from this reality that liturgical forms should take shape. The doctrine of the Trinity developed as the Church worshipped God through the Son and in the Spirit, and our hope is that its centrality will be realised anew in worship.

5.1.3 Similar questions must be asked of the relation between trinitarian theology and our conception of the kind of entity that the Church is. Again, we shall not solve all problems simply intellectually. But the shape our institutions take is partly dependent upon the expectations we have of the kind of entities that they are. In this case, our deliberations have led us to ask whether the Church has been thought sufficiently in the light of the Trinity, and whether questions about its institutional origins and legal unity have not rather predominated. In particular, it would appear that all churches tend to justify their own arrangements, and that here there is a crying need for ecumenical conversation. As one of our papers asked, '*Can* any one Christian communion produce, from within its own history and life, a comprehensive account of the nature of the church?' Another related matter of great ecumenical importance is the relation between the local and the universal Church. It might be argued that a strong stress on the unity of God may lead to an excessively centralizing view of the Church, and it was asked whether the Second Vatican Council, for all the progress it made in developing a more dynamic ecclesiology, gave adequate place to the local as distinct from the universal Church. Equally important, we need trinitarian controls on the ecclesiological imagery we use, if it is not to produce one-sided distortions. But it must be *trinitarian* theology as a whole that we use, not unconsidered appeals to persons of the Trinity. Suggestions we considered were that "Father-only" images are associated with power-lust and domination; "Jesus-only" images with

28

moralistic activism or individualistic pietism; "Spirit-only" images with introspective escapism or charismatic excess. We would not necessarily agree with the precise form in which such points are made, particularly in view of the fact that matters of causality in these matters are notoriously difficult to discern. But we do in general agree that conceptions of the Church derived from attention to one person of the Trinity only do tend to give rise to a variety of spiritual ills. As we have seen, in the being of God, Father, Son and Spirit are what they are only by virtue of their relations with each other; does not our ecclesiology equally require attention to trinitarian *perichoresis?*

5.1.4 The heart of the matter is, once again, the relation between christology and pneumatology in our thought about the Church. A strong orientation to christology stresses the past historical and so institutional aspects of ecclesiology. It is at this point that our Eastern representatives expressed themselves most unhappy with Western thinking. A careful study of the ecclesiology of Vatican II, for example, reveals that ecclesiology is still constructed basically with christological material alone; it is only *after* that that the Spirit is brought into this structure to animate it. This is of immense importance in view of the fact that it is with the institutional aspects of the Church that moderns find so much difficulty. While undoubtedly the difficulties are partly the outcome of modern individualism, the elements of truth in suspicions of institutional religion derive from a proper concern that the Church should be a community before it is an institution. Here the importance of the Trinity is twofold. First, by stressing the fact that God's being consists in community, it asserts the theological priority of community over institution or anything impersonal. (The Church has always behaved worst when she has likened herself to an empire or understood herself as primarily a legal institution). The Church must cease to be looked on primarily as an institution and be treated as a *way of being.* The Church is primarily *communion,* i.e. a set of relationships making up a mode of being, exactly as is the case of the trinitarian God. Second, by stressing the action of the Spirit as of equal importance to that of the Son, it makes it possible to emphasize God's present as well as his past action in constituting the Church and along with this the eschatological, future oriented, dimensions of ecclesiology. The Church will thus cease to be regarded as a historically given reality – an institution – which is a provocation to freedom. She will be regarded at the same time as something constantly *constituted,* i.e. emerging out of the co-incidence and con-vergence of relationships freely established by the Spirit. Arguments of this kind are important ecumenically above all because they show that according to such a trinitarian criterion, all churches alike, Orthodox, Protestant and Catholic stand in need of renewal in the Spirit.

5.2 **The *Filioque* and the Unity of the Church.** Such considerations bring us directly to the relation of trinitarian questions to the unity of the Church. One of the central focuses of schism between East and West, still at the centre of discussion, has been the *Filioque:* the addition to the original Niceno-Constantinopolitan creed affirming that the Spirit 'proceeds from the Father *and the Son*'. The dispute between the churches over the expression came to a head in the ninth century, when the ecclesiastical division was between Rome and Constantinople, on the one hand, and the Frankish church, which wished to make the *Filioque* canonical, on the other. It was as a result of later German influence in Rome that the Western church as a whole insisted, a century later, on the inclusion in the creed of the confession of belief in the 'double procession' of the Holy Spirit. It is one of the encouraging features of more recent discussion between the churches that the question is being discussed openly again. (See especially the volume edited by Lucas Vischer, details in the Appendix). What is involved in the dispute? Is it merely a matter of political power and institutional jealousies, or is more at stake? Once again, our enquiries reveal that at the root of the dispute between East and West, obscured though it has often been by less worthy motives, is the matter of personal being.

5.2.2 The importance of the *Filioque* can be approached on two levels, the economic – the way we conceive the Spirit to operate in the history of salvation; and the immanent – the implications of our conception of the Spirit for our notion of the being and nature of God. At the economic level, it can be said that some of the participants in our discussions believe that the relentlessly christological emphasis of much Western theology has tended to obscure the work of the Spirit. Some of us would want to put the matter more carefully, and say that it is the form that christology has taken that is the problem. What has been lacking is parallel to what we saw to be absent from Western ecclesiology, the conception of an intrinsic connection between the Holy Spirit and the person of Christ. That is ironic in view of the fact that the *Filioque* implies a very close relation between the two, but the outcome has been that either the institution or human consciousness has tended to take the place of the Spirit in much theology. Equally, the teaching that the Spirit comes from both the Father and the Son tends to undervalue the work of the Spirit by making him appear to be secondary to the Son. One outcome, as has already been suggested (3.1.3), is that certain important features of the Gospel narratives cease to shape the way we think of Jesus. In the Gospel of Luke, for example, there is in the account of the conception of Jesus a strong stress on the instrumentality of the Spirit in what took place. Similarly, we shall not appreciate such features of the story as the temptation if we fail to notice that Jesus does not resist because of some inbuilt perfection, but because he is empowered by the Spirit. This is, of course, a repetition of the point made above that much Western theology understresses the humanity of Jesus in general because it places too much weight on his relation to the eternal Word, so that it sometimes seems, in contradiction of the gospel stories, that his humanity is unreal, simply a cipher. By contrast, to hold that the Spirit has a crucial part in empowering the true humanity of Jesus helps us to escape our historical imbalance and to prevent us from holding that Jesus' divinity and humanity are contradictory predicates.

5.2.3 The dominance of christology over pneumatology in our interpretation of God's working in the world emerges also in what is often held to be a weakness of the theology of the Spirit in the West, where the Spirit sometimes appears to be little more than an appendage of Christ. There appears to be a pressure operating which prevents the tradition from giving the Spirit adequate personal weight. In Barth, for example, as one of our papers claimed, 'pneumatology is totally dominated by christology and indeed to speak of the Spirit is simply to speak of the extension of the power of Jesus Christ into the subjective sphere.' It seems likely that much contemporary inadequacy derives in large measure from St Augustine's doctrine of the Spirit as *vinculum caritatis*, where he seems to be reduced to a relationship between the other two, rather than seen as himself personal. Does this matter? It has already been argued in this report that an inadequate grasp of its trinitarian basis creates serious problems for our understanding of the Church. May it not similarly be true that an incapacity to give adequate content to the doctrine of the Spirit will make it difficult for us to discern the eschatological working of the Spirit in the world, for example in the cry for humanity on the part of the oppressed. Similarly, our doctrine of the Spirit will affect our understanding of the movement of history, and guarantee that it has an eschatological dimension.

5.2.4 Unless the Spirit is recognised as a distinct divine person, his work in the world will not be discerned as truly that of God. The question here centres on the difference between West and East, for both agree that the Spirit is God, while both tend to hold that the other fails to give adequate account of the nature of that divinity. We have already seen that major theologians of the Western tradition, St Augustine and Barth, appear to be unable to give an adequate account of the reality of the Spirit. If our argument so far is correct, it suggests that there are weaknesses in the way that the doctrine of God has developed. We are now, ecumenically, at a stage when anathemas have ceased and we are able to look coolly at the problems. At the centre there seems to be one question in the light of which the others can be understood. It is the matter which we have met at several stages of this report: whether reality is at bottom the creation of a personal God or the logical outworking of an impersonal principle. The argument goes something like this. Suppose that we accept the traditional Western position that the Spirit proceeds from the Father *and the Son (Filioque)*. Not only does the subordination of the Spirit to the Son, of which much has already been made in this report, appear to eventuate, but we appear to be faced with a further question. If the Spirit comes from two sources, is there a further principle of unity, underlying and accounting for the two? The fact is that not only is the human mind certain to look beyond the unresolved duality for a principle of unity underlying it, but that theologically it is bound to do so, if it is serious in finding the basis for all things in the reality of God. The majority of Western theologians have tended to look beyond the threeness of the persons to an underlying divine being or substance, and the effect has been to base the *persons* in an underlying *impersonal* substance or substratum. The outcome is that the basis of reality is something impersonal, with all the problems, and particularly the West's chronic tendency to modalism, that it involves. And behind that technical trinitarian concept, there lies a further question. Modalism implies that the real God lies hidden behind the modes of his historical manifestations, and so is essentially unknown. May not the roots of modern atheism lie in this very failure of the Christian tradition to think the reality of the personal God on the basis of the economy of creation and salvation – of where God actually relates to the world? The question which the East asks the West in this connection is: to what extent is Western theology tied to the idea of the priority of substance – and we might gloss impersonal substance – in God's being? Once again, we are pointed to the question of the way in which human and personal values are rooted in the way the world is.

5.2.5 The question that now arises is whether the denial of the *Filioque* would help to solve that particular problem. Two related points are made in this connection. The first is that, as we have already seen, the being of God must be conceived not to be some*thing* underlying the threeness of the persons but that which the three persons are in their relatedness to each other. The second is that we should base the being of God not in abstract *deity* but in the Father, who as a person provides a personal basis for the unity both of the deity and of all things.

The second of these claims is more difficult for Western minds because it appears to introduce a hierarchical grading into the deity, subordinating the Son and the Spirit to the Father in an almost Arian way. Against the necessity of drawing such a conclusion there are two main arguments. The first is derived from the concept of being with which we are operating, according to which the three are one in being, and therefore in deity, but distinguished in the way in which they are ordered to one another as originated and derived. At the heart of the matter is the concept of *taxis* or order with which we are working. It does not follow that a 'subordination', an 'ordering below' entails an inferiority of personhood, dignity or being. It often appears so to us because – for example – obedience is often a merely external relation rather than a hearing stemming from love. As Christians, however, we would want to argue to the contrary, that Jesus' humiliation, whether we see that demonstrated in his birth, his washing of the disciples' feet or his sacrificial death, is a mark of his divinity and glory, not of his inferiority. (The same applies in the case of human value and dignity, as Christians are often concerned to point out.) The second argument is from Scripture, which tends, when it speaks of God *tout court*, so to speak, to mean God the Father. It is the Father 'from whom are all things', the Son 'through whom are all things' (1 Cor. 8.6). Similarly, the Father initiates the economy of creation, and to him everything is directed (1 Cor. 15.23ff). On such a conception, the Son's and the Spirit's actions in the world are those of the 'two hands of God' (St Irenaeus), sent by the Father to do his work in the world. But this 'subordination', if such it be, is, as we have seen, in no way inimical to the conception that they are one in being with the Father. Questions such as this will recur when we turn, below (6) to the implications of trinitarian theology for moral and social questions such as those raised by feminism.

5.2.6 Even if we accept the foregoing argument, it does not follow that we should simply deny what the Western tradition has sought to express by its use of the *Filioque*. To show the underlying reason for its introduction, we shall begin with the chief Western objection to the Eastern way of conceiving the Trinity. The teaching that the Spirit proceeds from the Father alone on the immanent level can easily lead to a by-passing of the Son on the economic level and to a Spirit-centred mysticism, to which the person of Christ can easily become peripheral. That allusion to Barth's defence of the *Filioque* takes us to the strength of the Western position, which is that the New Testament does assert a close connection between the Son and the Spirit on the economic level. If, then, the doctrine of the immanent Trinity is to be true to Scripture, it is reasonable to conclude that any teaching about the immanent Trinity should take due account of the connectedness of Son and Spirit in the economy. The Western position, that is to say, can be taken to serve as a safeguard against speculation about the being of God which is unrelated to the way in which he is made known to us in Scripture. The Study Commission therefore wishes to dissociate itself from the suggestion that is sometimes made that all the ills of Western theology derive from the *Filioque* and that there is no case at all for the doctrine. We do, however, wish to acknowledge the fact that in ecumenical discussions there is a movement towards a consensus that the expression should be removed from the formal credal expressions of Christian belief. We believe that the removal should be made not for merely diplomatic reasons, but in order to give all the churches of divided Christendom the freedom to penetrate to the underlying questions which are at stake. We would like, that is to say, to play our part in bringing about a meeting of minds which will enable true ecumenical conversation to develop.

6 The Trinity, the Church and the World

6.1 **The Trinity and the Church's Teaching about Salvation.**
Another difference between East and West is revealed in an examination of their teaching about salvation. The West has tended to stress matters of sin, atonement and forgiveness, the East 'divinisation', the fulfilment of all created being in Christ. We might say that the West has developed the legal, the East the cosmic, dimensions of salvation. The distinction, however, can be exaggerated, in that a founder of Eastern soteriology like St Athanasius has given a central place to the doctrine of sin, while in the West St Anselm paid attention to the cosmic dimensions of the divine justice, a stress increased in this century in an influential study of the Atonement by Gustaf Aulen. We have sought to explore something of the relation between the Atonement and the Trinity as it bears upon our understanding of God and of the central Christian claim that in the life, death and resurrection of Jesus God is at work to forgive, restore and complete his creation. It must however be confessed that our deliberations were somewhat inconclusive, and that only a few general points can be made here.

6.1.2 At the centre of recent difficulties with the doctrine of the Atonement has been part of the tradition's tendency to a dualistic presentation of God's work in salvation. The dualism takes two related forms. In the first there is a breach between the roles attributed to the Son and the Father. It has sometimes appeared that the work of the Son is an appeasing or 'buying off' of the Father, with the result that God sometimes appears to be a God who punishes the human race through visiting his wrath upon Jesus. The second form of the same dualism is to be found in the distinction between the God made known in the economy of salvation, and particularly the cross, and God as he is in himself. Both forms introduce a breach in the fabric of reality, and throw salvation into doubt by making it appear that the 'real' God is radically other than the one who is active for human salvation in the life, death and resurrection of Jesus. Members of the Study Commission are agreed that the solution to the problems consequent upon this dualism is to be found in the doctrine of the Trinity, where there is taught the oneness of Father and Son in the communion of the Spirit. But there have been differences about where that oneness is to be found and how it is to be understood.

6.1.3 One possibility which was examined (and which owes a good deal to the theology of Jürgen Moltmann) is to affirm that salvation is brought about by the suffering of God the Father no less than that of the Son in the event of the cross. On such a conception, the whole Trinity participates in human suffering in order to create human response to God and human participation in the divine life. The outcome is the removal of dualism by means of a much nearer, though not complete, identification of the immanent with the economic Trinity. The being of God can be thought about only as act or event, characterised by movements of relationship which are disclosed in, and affected by, the event of Christ and his cross. This approach claims that to speak of God as 'act' only makes sense in terms of human *participation* in the relationships of Father, Son and Spirit; thus, there can be no concept of God which does not include humankind within the fellowship of the divine life, though it is stressed that God has himself chosen to be like this. The objections to this approach, which on the whole appeared stronger to most members of the group than its advantages, were that it achieved too close an identification of economic with immanent Trinity, so that the freedom of God which is so essential a feature of Christian teaching about salvation was endangered; and that it lost the drama of interchange between God and humankind in Christ, and with it the historical centrality of the cross as both salvation and judgement. For those who maintained these objections, the key to the matter was to pay greater attention to the part played by the person of the Holy Spirit in relation to Jesus. We have seen already (above 3.1) that the Spirit is crucial in christology, because Jesus is the one who receives the Spirit and exercises his ministry in his strength. In relation to the doctrine of the Atonement, the point needs to be extended, so that we can say that it is through the Spirit that Jesus is enabled to achieve the work of the Father, which is the salvation of the world. It is in this way that any dualism between the work of the Father and that of the Son is avoided.

6.2 **Salvation, the Trinity and Politics.** Recent years have seen an increase of interest in the social and political dimensions of salvation, partly in an attempt to correct over-individualist tendencies in the past. They have also witnessed an awareness that Christianity has been used to provide legitimation for particular political systems, sometimes evil ones. We have already alluded to the argument of one German theologian during the Nazi era that monistic theologies tend to legitimate totalitarian regimes, while trinitarian theologies the opposite. Recent historical studies, however, have suggested that it is not easy to draw direct lines between theological positions and political theories. We therefore wish to proceed with great caution in this matter, but none the less to explore the implications that the being of God as triune has for the social and political institutions in which human life takes shape, just as it bears in important ways upon the being of the Church as community.

6.2.2 The chief thing to be said is that it is a political statement for the Church simply to be the Church. As the social reality that she is called to be, a community whose centre should be love rather than coercion, she presents all political systems with a question about their authenticity. All political systems, whether individualist or collectivist in orientation, are in danger of ceasing to treat persons as persons. By contrast, as one of our papers put it, 'to speak of the Holy Trinity as persons is to affirm God in Trinity, the unlimited and timeless love of three persons in ec-static self-giving to one another, as primary to the understanding of our world also. Persons come before concepts . . .' That is not to suggest that churches are immune from behaving coercively or from forming their being in the image of an alien political theory; but that the Church's calling is so to hold the Trinity in the centre that she will continue to be a reminder to society of its true nature.

6.2.3 We have argued above (5.1) that it is one of the weaknesses of the way in which ecclesiology has developed that the Church has often understood herself after the model of political institutions rather than as a community. In times when the Church is rightly involving herself in political matters, we believe that it is essential for Christians to discuss politics in relation to the doctrine of the Trinity. The chief reason for this is that there is a danger that the Church will appear to be, and may in fact be, no more than one more secular player or interest group among the many who seek to wield power and influence. If the doctrine of the Trinity is held in the centre, we are more likely to hold to that which this report has already argued to be the heart of the matter, the priority of persons, and that means persons in community, over all other considerations. It is here that we shall be best able to contribute a distinctive voice to political debate, while at the same time calling attention to the dimensions of human polity that are both centrally important and most likely to be forgotten in the strife of competing interests.

6.3 The Fatherhood of God and the Question of Feminism.

The chief feminist arguments against the doctrine of the Trinity derive from the apparently implied maleness of the deity. If God is known as Father, then it appears that he is also male, and therefore we endorse a form of patriarchy. Not only does this appear to exclude more than half of the human race from being truly in the image of God, but in practice it fosters oppression, male domination and other ills consequent upon elevating one sex at the expense of the other. As one of our papers put it, 'the thoughtless and careless use of male imagery about God has an actively oppressive effect, and leaves many people feeling that they cannot love or be loved by such a God'.

6.3.2 We do not wish to deny the elements of truth in the arguments that have been mentioned; but neither do we wish to concede that they damage the heart of or the necessity for a trinitarian doctrine of God. How, then, should the arguments be treated? One tempting riposte, particularly for those unsympathetic to the feminist case, is to appeal to 'tradition'. Such an appeal would argue that Christianity is what it is by virtue of its trinitarian heritage; and to reject the arguments of – say – the Fathers is to deny essential Christianity, and to turn the faith into something else. There is something in that argument. From the earliest times, Christianity has been a faith that is 'handed down' from one generation to another. If one were to introduce a radical break into the tradition, it would indeed be to throw the whole into question. However, such a riposte would not be adequate, for at least two reasons. The first is that our opponent is likely to reply that the outcome is so much the worse for tradition, because if the tradition is simply used in an authoritarian manner to defend the indefensible, it is itself called radically into question. The second reason is the ambiguity of *tradition*. For example, some would claim that it is the feminist case which represents the true development of the tradition, so that far from introducing a break, it is developing its true implications. Thus it can be argued that many modern uses of the concept of fatherhood represent usages foreign to its biblical origins. The argument must not therefore be seen as a straightforward one of 'traditionalists' against 'radicals'. Both sides are concerned with the way in which the Christian tradition has taken and should take shape.

6.3.3 We shall approach the question with the help of a discussion of language. Here, a number of different points can be made. The first is that it is a mistake to treat the word *father* simply as a general notion or image that we project upon God. If that were so, it would be equally valid to project images of motherhood. We do not, however, believe that trinitarian theology is that kind of enterprise, and one of our papers argued that a (general) 'concept of the fatherhood of God' is the product of a nineteenth century school which as a matter of fact falsified the tradition. It is not a matter of playing abstract and general concepts or models against one another, but of finding and defining the words which least inadequately express what we need to say. A second argument concerns the language of the Bible. In the Old Testament, God is rarely called Father, and then usually in contexts of nurturing and fostering, rather than in those associated with the attributes and behaviour our society has come to label masculine. In the New Testament, the word is not introduced as an image or concept, but relationally, and primarily in connection with the relation between Jesus and his Father. This links with a third, and very important point, that we cannot lightly toss aside the linguistic context which encapsulates the content of the Gospel. We have been reminded of the words of St Athanasius, that the only reason we have for calling God Father is that he is so named in Scripture. That is not to be understood as an authoritarian and merely biblicist appeal, but as calling attention to the historical shape which the gospel as a matter of fact took. If such an ascription were further taken to imply that God is male, that would be an improper inference. A similar point could be made christologically. That Jesus was a man does not entail the maleness of the eternal Son. We believe that it is a contingent fact that the Word of God was incarnate in a man. It did not have to be so, but given that God so acted, we cannot do other than receive the tradition on its basis. We agree that exclusively male imagery has actively oppressive effects, and that fatherhood can be the legitimation of the misogynist, but we do not believe that the language of fatherhood is meant to be understood in that way. There has been far too much misogyny in the Christian tradition, and it is, we believe, a denial of what we see to be the true implications of the trinitarian gospel. The fatherhood of God needs to be liberated from the cultural repression of male dominated societies. The fourth point is that, along with all language which is employed to speak of the being of God, the word *father* is to be construed apophatically, that is, by means of a determined 'thinking away' of the inappropriate – and in this context, that means masculine – connotations of the term. (For the same reason we do not believe that it is a solution to suppose one person of the Trinity to be female). What will remain will be an orientation to personhood, to being in relation involving origination in a personal sense, not maleness. It may be that here again the Western tradition has exacerbated its problems by its effective binitarianism. By concentrating excessive attention on the Father-Son relationship it has tended to neglect the fact that we are here concerned with the communion of three persons. As we have argued above (4.3), an anthropology developed upon trinitarian foundations will suggest a teaching of the image of God oriented to the notion of community, and specifically to one taking shape in our co-humanity as women and men.

6.4 **Christianity and Other Religions.** The matter of the Trinity in relation to the relationships of Christians with people of other faiths can be approached with a number of different assumptions. On the one hand, it can be argued that to hold to the doctrine of the Trinity presents an initial barrier to conversation, so that, particularly in relation to other monotheistic faiths, it should be kept in the background or even abandoned as positively harmful. The members of the Commission have not for the most part found this to be a fruitful approach. We do, however, acknowledge, that there are in the past behaviour of the Church historical grounds for suspicion, in that the doctrine has often been used as the basis of the rejection and anathematizing of other human beings who are no less than we the objects of God's love. An over-dogmatic particularism, therefore, should be avoided, although it has to be admitted that any particularism will not be without its difficulties in creating stumbling blocks between representatives of different faiths.

6.4.2 Some of us feel that, in view of the urgent need for the Christian Church to witness to and work for the unity of humankind, more stress should be laid on the experiences which we have in common with other believers. On the other hand, most of us argue that unless we acknowledge our differences from others, we shall not be able to approach them honestly. We seek to find in trinitarian doctrine, in our beliefs about the very being of God, the foundation for the unity of humankind. If this latter is the correct means of approach, the question remains of whether the doctrine is simply a *given* to be taken account of and, where necessary modified as the result of conversations with others; or whether it has positive implications for the way in which the task of conversation is to be approached. A number of different views were represented and expressed in the Commission's discussions. Some held firmly that it should not be assumed without question that dialogue was the primary issue at stake, but that, for example, the identity and integrity of Christianity was of greater importance. Another view was that we can find in trinitarian doctrine resources for approaching, in the context of discussions with members of other faiths, the question of monotheism, already adumbrated in 3.2 above. If monotheism – not simply the matter of the unity of God, but of *what kind of unity* – is an important question for our understanding of the kind of world in which we live and of the values we espouse within it, then it is essential that we face openly the differences between different conceptions of the divine unity. While it is right that we should take seriously and, where appropriate, with due penitence, the charges made by members of other faiths against the way our theology has sometimes been used oppressively, we should not be afraid to face seriously the differences between trinitarian and other forms of monotheism. The Trinity teaches us that unity should be conceived personally and relationally, not logically and mathematically (and therefore impersonally). In this context it may be asked whether the failures of the Church have been due not so much to the doctrine of the Trinity as to our failure to think trinitarianly enough. Here, the Study Commission believes that it has only begun to think through some of the positive implications of this aspect of trinitarian thought, and hopes that its suggestions will be taken as an invitation for further exploration.

6.4.3 Most positively, we would wish to recommend that Christians look beyond a merely intellectual solution to the problem of the relation between trinitarian Christianity and other religions. The intellectual questions are indeed important, but we wish to urge an approach which begins with our common humanity. All are in search of true personhood, the personhood which we believe is the gift of the eschatological Spirit. In trinitarian theology there are resources which can be employed to point to the place where personhood can be found. At the centre of all our concerns has been the matter of relationship. Because God's being consists in what the three persons give to and receive from each other, we know that our humanity is to be found only in our being in relation, as forms of community are realised in which we human beings live *for* and *with* each other. That is a claim which Christians can teach and practice without causing needless offence to those who do not share our particular beliefs. Equally, it should teach us that we are not being truly 'personal' if we do not listen to what others have to say to and about us. A similar point can be made about worship. Christians do indeed worship in a way focussed by our trinitarian beliefs, but if worship rather than intellectual polemics is the centre of our lives, we are more likely to listen than simply to assert or argue.

6.4.4 Such teaching and the practice to which it leads should mean that Christians are not unduly dismissive of or deaf to the contentions of those who do not share our faith. This is particularly important in our relations with Jews and Muslims, for both Christianity and Islam have roots in Judaism and share the common monotheism witnessed by the Hebrew Scriptures. All alike wish to maintain faith in the God of Abraham and Isaac, and it is much to be regretted that a history of polemics rather than dialogue has divided us. Despite this we believe that there is bound to be a difference between our attitude to members of other faiths and to other Christians. We cannot without loss of integrity, indeed loss of the trinitarian vision, deny our faith that in Christ and the Spirit is to be found the new humanity to which all are moving. It is only on that basis that we can approach those outside the Christian fold, including adherents of non-theistic religions and ways of life, in the confidence that there is a common humanity on the basis of which we can meet them as brothers and sisters, children of one Father.

7 Conclusions

7.1   As will be apparent from the body of the report, we believe that, although we have not taken every question that could be raised in trinitarian theology, nevertheless the matters we have considered are of wide-ranging importance. Negatively, we conclude that the neglect of the doctrine of the Trinity has led to serious consequences for the life of the people of God, and therefore for the world in which its life is lived. Of particular significance is the way in which the neglect has occasioned serious shortcomings in the way the life of the Church has been understood and has taken shape. Renewed attention to the Trinity would, we believe, assist in a process in which the Church could become a true community of men and women, called together by the Holy Spirit, to the praise of God in worship and life.

7.2   Ecumenically, we believe that the doctrine of the Trinity has much to contribute to the process in which the divided churches of Christendom are drawing near to one another. The unity of Christians will be achieved as we gather in worship in the communion of the Holy Spirit. Attention to formulations is secondary, but is none the less important, partly because it is often formulations which have divided us. Here, one specific recommendation we would make is that the churches of the West should remove the *Filioque* from their confessions of belief. As we have said already, we believe that, far from involving a loss of integrity, such an initiative would open the way to a creative exploration of the common basis of our faith.

7.3   Equally positively, we believe that the doctrine of the Trinity has important contributions to make to the life of the world. In a world widely thought to be empty or hostile to human life, we believe the Church's proclamation of the basis and end of all things in the love of a personal God to be of incalculable value. In face of political systems which threaten either to set one person against all others or to swallow up everyone in an impersonal mass society, we likewise wish to commend a teaching which asserts both the importance of each particular person and the interdependence of all upon one another, and that the fulfilment of human beings is to be found in relationships in community and not in self-assertive individualism. Anthropologically, we believe that conceptions of our co-humanity, grounded in the community of Father, Son and Spirit, have much to contribute to the great questions of our time about relations between the sexes and between members of different religious communions.

7.4 We wish, therefore, to commend to the churches and to the society which they serve not only the results of our studies, which have been a great enrichment to us all, but that to which they point, the God made known to the world through Jesus and the Spirit as Father, Son and Holy Spirit, a God whose being consists in communion. We therefore wish to return to the confession of the centrality of worship with which the main body of this report began. The Christian response to God is above all to be found in lives of praise and worship. We have written much about the importance of the person, and wish to conclude by affirming that we are most truly human – must truly personal – when at the eucharist we participate, through the Spirit, in the communion that is Christ's relation to the Father. Our concern here is not with abstract teaching – though we do not wish to deny the importance of teaching – but with life: with the life that is the eternal communion of God, Father, Son and Holy Spirit; and with the human life in communion with God that is God's gift through the incarnation of the Son in our flesh and the sending of the Spirit to realise in our present age the blessings of the age to come.

8 Appendix: Recent Writing on the Trinity

The following bibliography indicates that theologians with a wide range of positions are becoming aware of the importance of the doctrine of the Trinity. James Mackey, whose approach is strongly experiential, is of the writers listed the one most sceptical of the usefulness of trinitarian categories. Roman Catholics like Rahner and Kasper are strongly trinitarian, though in many ways highly critical of the form Western trinitarianism has sometimes taken. Moltmann stresses the political and ecclesiological importance of a revised trinitarianism, while Zizioulas is both critical of some manifestations of his own Orthodox tradition and insistent on the importance of the Cappadocian approach to the Trinity for the life of church and culture.

Historical-critical questions about the justification of the doctrine of the Trinity for the Bible are discussed in Brown, Hill, Kasper and Wainwright.

1. The fountainheads of recent discussion of the Trinity are:

Karl Barth — *Church Dogmatics I/1*. E.T. by G.W. Bromiley, Edinburgh: T & T Clark, 1975

Vladimir Lossky — *The Mystical Theology of the Eastern Church*. Cambridge and London: James Clarke, 1957

Karl Rahner — *The Trinity*. E.T. by J. Donceel, London: Burns and Oates, 1970

2. Other recent works:

David Brown — *The Divine Trinity*. London: Duckworth, 1985

Yves Congar — *I Believe in the Holy Spirit*. 3 Vols. E.T. by David Smith, London: Geoffrey Chapman, 1983

E.J. Fortman — *Theological Resources – The Triune God*. London: Hutchinson, 1972

Colin E. Gunton — *Enlightenment and Alienation. An Essay Towards a Trinitarian Theology*. London: Marshall, Morgan and Scott, 1985

Martin Hengel	*The Son of God.* London: SCM Press, 1976
Alasdair Heron	*The Holy Spirit. The Holy Spirit in the Bible, in the History of Christian Thought and in recent Theology.* London: Marshall, Morgan and Scott, 1983
William J. Hill	*Three Personed God. The Trinity as a Mystery of Salvation.* Washington: Catholic University of America Press, 1982
Robert W. Jenson	*The Triune Identity.* Philadelphia: Fortress Press, 1982
Eberhard Jüngel	*The Doctrine of the Trinity.* Edinburgh: Scottish Academic Press, 1976
C.B. Kaiser	*The Doctrine of God. An Historical Survey.* London: Marshall, Morgan and Scott, 1982
Walter Kasper	*The God of Jesus Christ,* E.T. by M. J. O'Connell, London: SCM Press, 1984
G. W. Lampe	*God as Spirit.* Oxford: Clarendon Press, 1977
Sallie McFague	*Metaphorical Theology:* Models of God in Religious Language. London: SCM Press, 1983
Sallie McFague	*Models of God:* Theology for an Ecological Nuclear Age. London: SCM Press, 1987
James Mackey	*The Christian Experience of God as Trinity.* London: SCM Press, 1983
John MacMurray	*Persons in Relation.* London: Faber, 1961
E.L. Mascall	*The Triune God. An Ecumenical Study.* Worthing: Churchman Publishing, 1986
Jürgen Moltmann	*The Trinity and the Kingdom of God. The Doctrine of God.* E.T. by M. Kohl, London: SCM Press, 1981
Lesslie Newbigin	*The Open Secret.* London: SPCK, 1978
John O'Donnell	*Trinity and Temporality: the Christian Doctrine of God in the Light of Process Theology and the Theology of Hope.* Oxford University Press, 1983
John O'Donnell	*The Mystery of the Triune God.* London: Sheed and Ward, 1988

Thomas A. Smail	*The Forgotten Father*. London: Hodder and Stoughton, 1980
Thomas A. Smail	*The Giving Gift. The Holy Spirit in Person*. London: Hodder and Stoughton, 1988
P. Toon and J.D. Spiceland (eds)	*One God in Trinity. An Analysis of the Primary Dogma of Christianity*. London: Bagster, 1980
T. F. Torrance (ed)	*Theological Dialogue between Orthodox and Reformed Churches*. Edinburgh and London: Scottish Academic Press, 1985
Lukas Vischer (ed)	*Spirit of God, Spirit of Christ. Ecumenical Reflections on the* Filioque *Controversy*. London: SPCK, 1981
Arthur W. Wainwright	*The Trinity in the New Testament*. London: SPCK, 2e, 1969
World Council of Churches Faith and Order Papers:	No. 104, *Confessing our Faith around the World I* (1980)
	No. 120, *Confessing our Faith around the World II* (1983)
	No. 123, *Confessing our Faith around the World III* (1984)
	No. 126, *Confessing our Faith around the World IV* (1985)
	No. 139, *One God, One Lord, One Spirit: On the Explication of the Apostolic Faith Today*, ed. Hans-Georg Link
	No. 140, *Confessing One Faith: Towards an Ecumenical Explication of the Apostolic Faith as Expressed in the Niceno-Constantinopolitan Creed (381): Study Document* (1987)
John D. Zizioulas	*Being as Communion. Studies in Personhood and the Church*. London: DLT, 1985

9 Members of the BCC Study Commission on Trinitarian Doctrine Today

Tony Brown — Religious Society of Friends
Mr Costa Carras — Orthodox: Co–Chairman
Dr Sarah Coakley — Church of England
Rev Dr Colin Davey — BCC staff: Secretary
Rev Dr Paul Fiddes — Baptist
Rev Prof Colin Gunton — United Reformed Church
Rev Canon Anthony Harvey — Church of England
Rev Prof Alasdair Heron — Church of Scotland
Rev Archimandrite Ephrem (Lash) — Orthodox
Rev Anthony Meredith S.J. — Roman Catholic
Rev Basil Osborne — Orthodox
Rev Tom Smail — Church of England
Very Rev Dr Philip Tartaglia — Roman Catholic
Rev Prof James Torrance — Church of Scotland: Co–Chairman
Rev Dr David Tripp — Methodist Church
Dr Andrew Walker — Orthodox
Ms Jane Williams — Church of England
Metropolitan John (Zizioulas) of Pergamon — Orthodox